Thus Spoke Khayyam

The Rubaiyat of Omar Khayyam

Translated by
Ayob Palani and Adnan Talabani

BALBOA
PRESS
A DIVISION OF HAY HOUSE

Balboa Press books may be ordered through booksellers or by contacting:

Balboa Press
A Division of Hay House
1663 Liberty Drive
Bloomington, IN 47403
www.balboapress.com.au
1-(877) 407-4847

ISBN: 978-1-4525-0741-5 (sc)
ISBN: 978-1-4525-0742-2 (e)

Because of the dynamic nature of the Internet, any web addresses or links contained in this book may have changed since publication and may no longer be valid. The views expressed in this work are solely those of the translator and do not necessarily reflect the views of the publisher, and the publisher hereby disclaims any responsibility for them.

The translator of this book does not dispense medical advice or prescribe the use of any technique as a form of treatment for physical, emotional, or medical problems without the advice of a physician, either directly or indirectly. The intent of the translator is only to offer information of a general nature to help you in your quest for emotional and spiritual well-being. In the event you use any of the information in this book for yourself, which is your constitutional right, the translator and the publisher assume no responsibility for your actions.

Printed in the United States of America

Balboa Press rev. date: 9/28/2012

A word from the Translators

The reason why we have taken the task of a new translation for the Rubaiyat of Omar Khayyam is because so far, the magnitude of his poetry have not been presented with a full consideration for his unique expression and usage of words.

Introduction

Umar ibn Ibrahim al-Khayyam Nishapur was born in Iran (1048-1131). He was a Persian polymath: philosopher, mathematician, astronomer and poet. He also wrote treatises on mechanics, geography, mineralogy, music, climatology and Islamic theology.

Nishapur, was the place of his birth, from an early age he went to Samarkand, and attained his education there. Bukhara is where afterwards he left to and there he became known and established himself as a mathematician and astronomers of the medieval period. On algebra he has become one of the most important authors before modern times, by writing, the Treatise on Demonstration of Problems of Algebra, the method includes in itself the geometric for solving cubic equations by intersecting a hyperbola with a circle, which he has contributed to a calendar reform.

Omar Khayyam besides his famous work the Rubaiyat and other significant scientific work, he has also done more works on philosophy and teaching but not have received great attention. And also it has been stated for decades that he was educating student with the teachings of ibn Sina (Avicenna) in Nishapur where Khayyám was born and buried and where his mausoleum today remains a masterpiece of Iranian architecture visited by many people every year.

Khayyam has had an impact not only in Iranian literature but also outside Iran and non-speaking countries. His popularization in Europe and especially in England, the translation of his work the Rubaiyat by Edward Fitzgerald have made him the most famous poet in the world, beside that, also Al-Zamakhshari referred to him as "the philosopher of the world".

Acknowledgement

First of all we would like to send our thanks and appreciation to some of the people that has had an impact on our understanding and translation of the Rubaiyat.

Ali Jafari the Persian poet and author, one of our close friend, has helped us a great deal, with his revisions and clarification of this book. We would like to mention here that in the 63rd quatrain, where it starts with (A cunning one I saw . . .) the Persian word "Kheng خنگ" consists of two meaning in Persian literature, one being "Stupid" and the other a "Horse", Ali Jafari has stated that the word here should be "Horse" we appreciate his view but we find the word "stupid" to go more closely to this quatrain, and we leave it for the reader to decide.

An a special thanks to those who indirectly have helped us taking on this task, Ahamd Shamloo, a famous Persian poet, writer and journalist, has encourage and helped us by his beautiful *Masterpiece* recitation of Omar Khayyam's poetry.

We want also send thanks to Hasha Palani for the Designing and also his help with some of the poems.

And also we send our thanks to the following sites which were a great help.

www.rhymer.com

www.dictonary-farsi.com

thesaurus.com

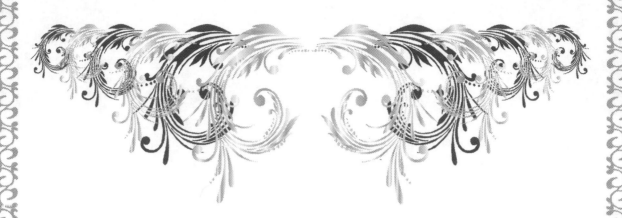

01

The mysteries of life, neither known by you nor I

The solving of this puzzle, neither known by you nor I

There is behind the curtain debate of you and I

As the curtain falls, neither you remain nor I

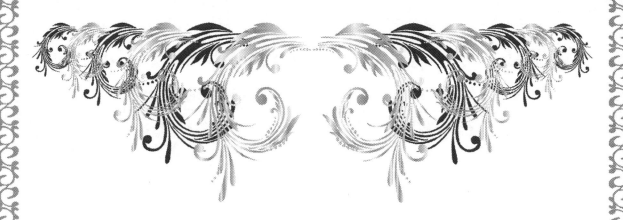

01

اسرار ازل را نه تو دانی و نه من

وین حل معما نه تو خوانی و نه من

هست از پس پرده گفت‌وگوی من و تو

چون پرده بر افتد نه تو مانی و نه من

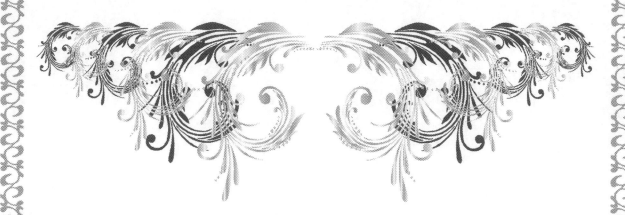

02

As the clouds of spring washed the tulip's semblance

Rise to a cup of wine, with the aim of sincere fragrance

This greenery that today, in perceiving you spends

Tomorrow all, from the soil of you ascends

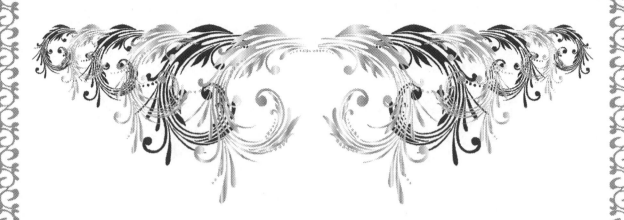

02

چون ابر به نوروز رخ لاله بشست

برخیز و به جام باده کن عزم درست

کین سبزه که امروز تماشا گه توست

فردا همه از خاک تو بر خواهد رست

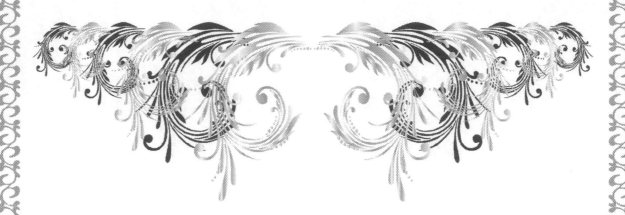

03

Away from pure wine to live, I cannot

Without liquor, to drag this body's weight, I cannot

I am enslaved to that moment

When cupbearer says, take another cup, I cannot

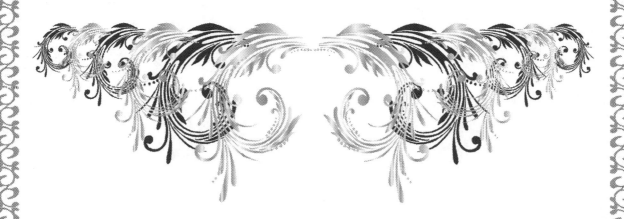

03

من به می ناب زیستن نتوانم

بی باده کشید بار تن نتوانم

من بنده آن دمم که ساقی گوید

یک جام دگر بگیر و من نتوانم

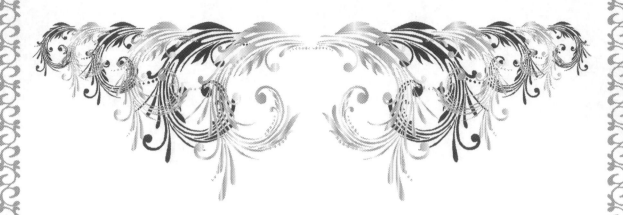

04

Devour wine, for that is the eternal life
That is the harvest your cycle of youth rife
The time of flower, liquor and lovers tipsy
Be happy for an instant that is what living envy

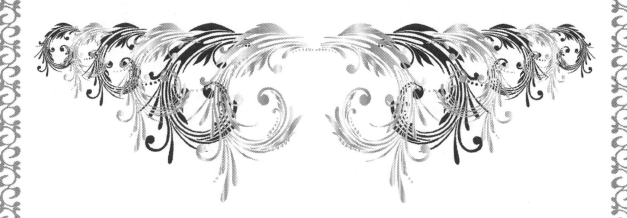

04

می نوش که عمر جاودانی این است

خود حاصلت از دور جوانی این است

هنگام گل و مل است و یاران سرمست

خوش باش دمی که زندگانی اینست

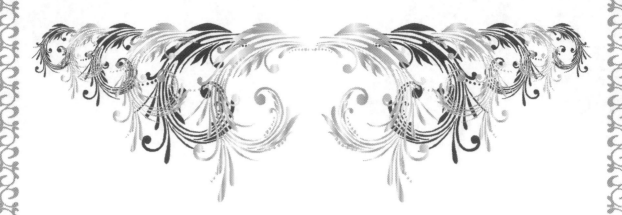

05

The instant of aurora, and the rooster of morn

Aware are you why, it keeps crowing in mourn

Means, is being manifested in the mirror of morning

Of life another night passed, and you unknowing

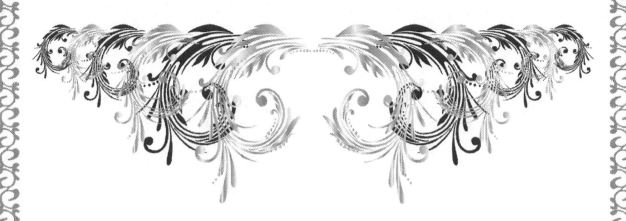

05

هنگام سپیده دم خروس سحری

دانی که چرا همی کند نوحه‌گری

یعنی که نمودند در آیینه صبح

کز عمر شبی گذشت و تو بی‌خبری

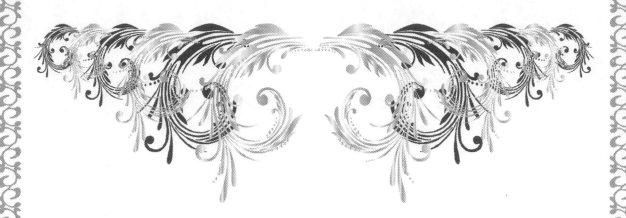

06

A while in childhood to master-hood we came

A while in master-hood joyous we became

Final word hearken, what have we had to gain

From dust we arise, taken by wind in vain

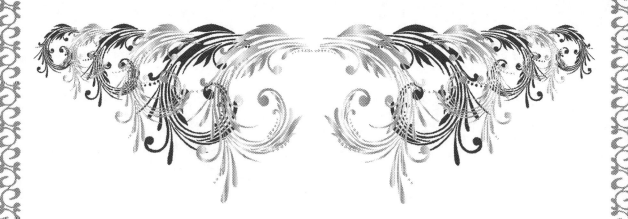

06

یک چند به کودکی به استاد شدیم

یک چند ز استادی خود شاد شدیم

پایان سخن شنو که ما را چه رسید

از خاک در آمدیم و برباد شدیم

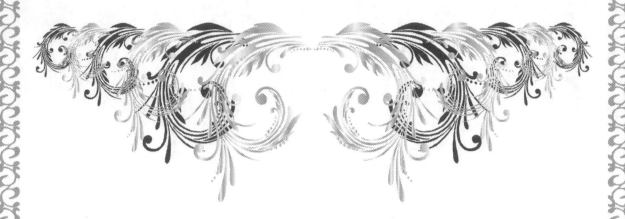

07

From my arrival for the universe, benefit did not produce

And in my departure, its greatness and majesty will not reduce

There is none to hearken for my ear's nerve

This arrival and departure what purpose did it serve

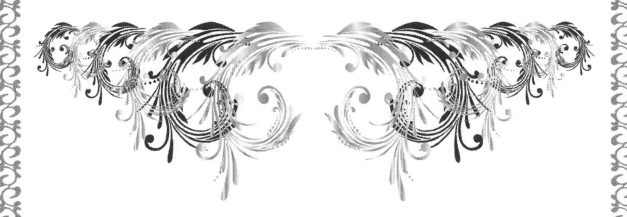

07

از آمدنم نبود گردون را سود

وز رفتن من جاه و جلالش نفزود

از هیچ کسی نیز دو گوشم نشنود

کین آمدن و رفتنم از بهر چه بود

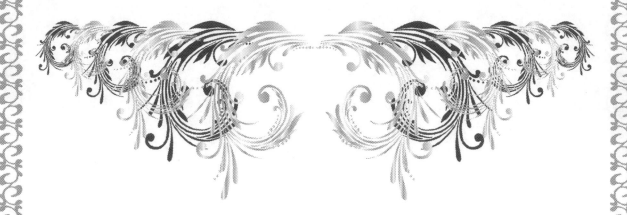

08

Look In the world, what have I emerged, naught

The harvest of life, what in my hand converged, naught

The enlighten candle I am, but as I extinguished, naught

I am the Holy Grail Cup, but as I shattered, naught

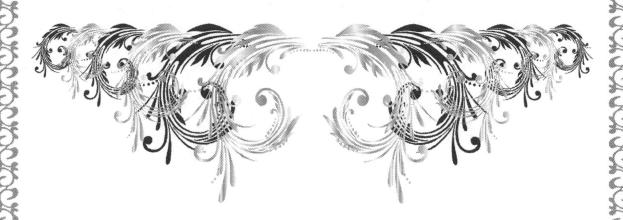

08

بنگر ز جهان چه طرف بربستم هیچ

وز حاصل عمر چیست در دستم هیچ

شمع طربم ولی چو بنشستم هیچ

من جام جمم ولی چو بشکستم هیچ

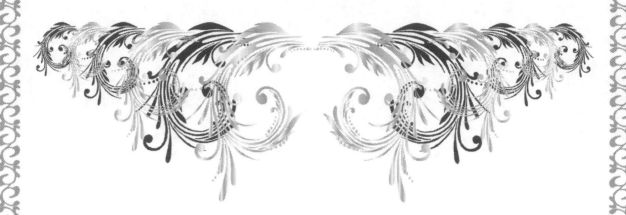

09

World by desire be it driven, end is what

This book of life be it re-read, end is what

Suppose to hearts longing, passes a hundred years

A hundred years more, be it passes, end is what

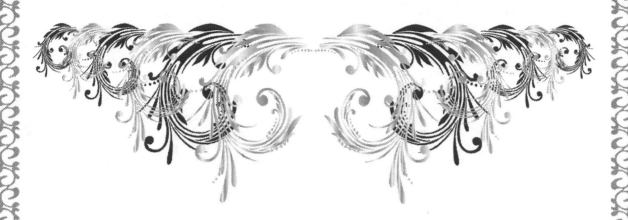

09

دنیا بمراد رانده گیر آخر چه

وین نامه عمر خوانده گیر آخر چه

گیرم که بکام دل بماندی صد سال

صد سال دگر بمانده گیر آخر چه

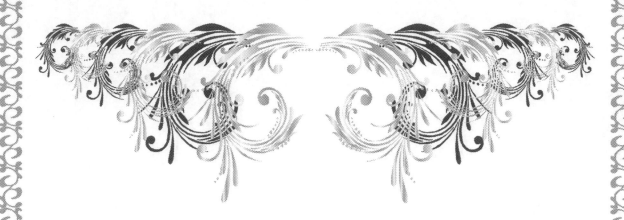

10

It's nothing, the world and everything you've observed

It's nothing, even that what you've said and heard

It's nothing, end to end the horizons you've sprinted

It's nothing, even that gliding in the house you've tasted

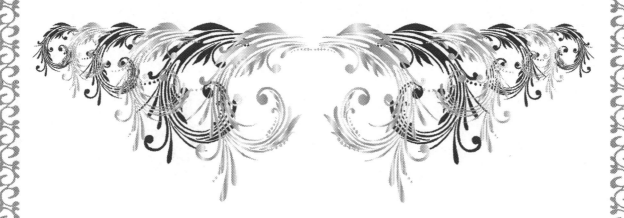

10

دنیا دیدی و هر چه دیدی هیچ است

و آن نیز که گفتی و شنیدی هیچ است

سرتاسر آفاق دویدی هیچ است

و آن نیز که در خانه خزیدی هیچ است

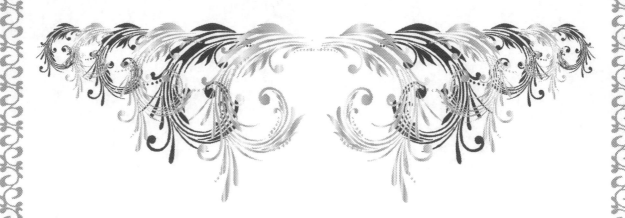

11

Oh lo, in vain we have withered away

By the capsized sphere's sickle, we abrade away

Woe, with pain and regret, till we got the eye blinked

Annihilated to the desires of self, we were extinct

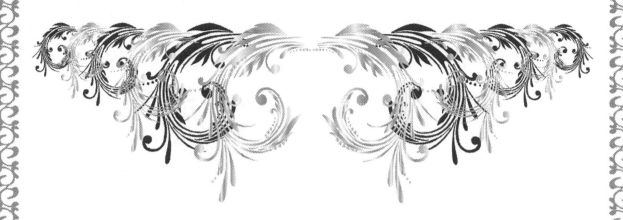

11

افسوس که بی فایده فرسوده شدیم

وز داس سپهر سرنگون سوده شدیم

دردا و ندامتا که تا چشم زدیم

نابوده به کام خویش نابوده شدیم

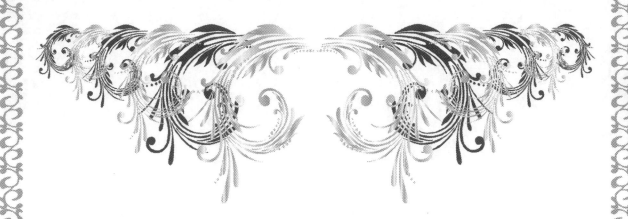

12

Be aware that the days bring forth a foul enticement

In comfort don't sit, the cycle's razor is a sharp tyrant

To your fancy if times almond pastry present

Be aware swallow not, for its a poison potent

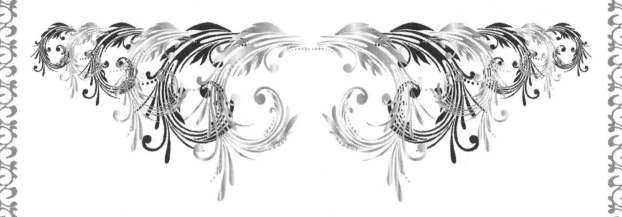

12

هشدار که روزگار شورانگیز است

ایمن منشین که تیغ دوران تیز است

در کام تو گر زمانه لوزینه نهد

زنهار فرو مبر که زهرآمیز است

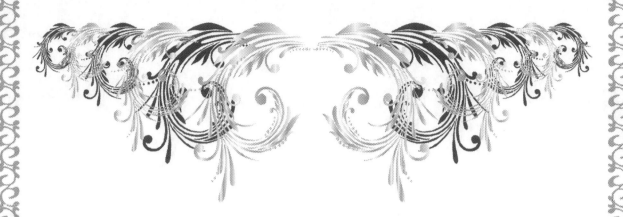

13

Day is grievance and the world an Utter tribulation

Sphere is all Plague and Cosmos is oppression

In sum up, as I look into the world's deed

Tranquil are no one, if there is, are few indeed

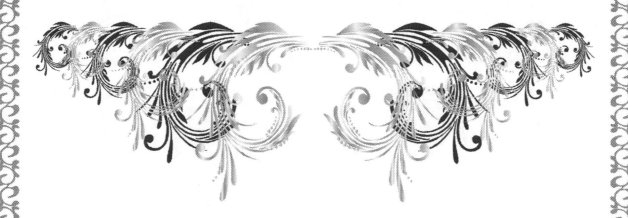

13

عالم همه محنتست و ایام غم است

گردون همه آفتست و گیتی ستم است

فی الجمله چو در کار جهان می نگرم

آسوده کسی نیست و گر هست کم است

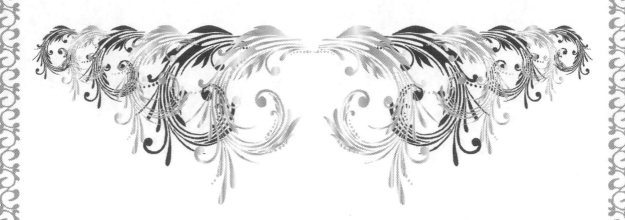

14

Before you are shocked by a Siege

Ordain yourself to a wine of prestige

Oh, ignorant dull, you are not gold

In Earth embedded, excavated, then be hold

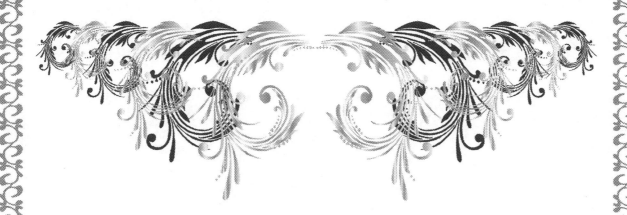

14

زان پیش که بر سرت شبیخون آرند

فرمای که تا باده گلگون آرند

تو زر نئی ای غافل نادان که ترا

در خاک نهند و باز بیرون آرند

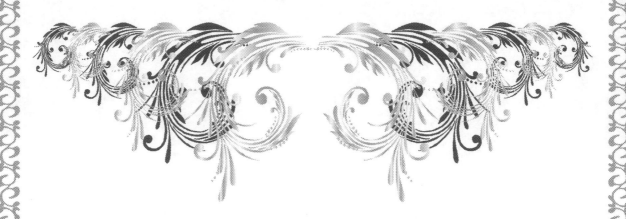

15

In the pot maker's shop, I was a while ago
I Saw two thousands pots, convey in mute aglow
Each one by words in surreal said to me
Where the pot maker, pot buyer, pot seller be

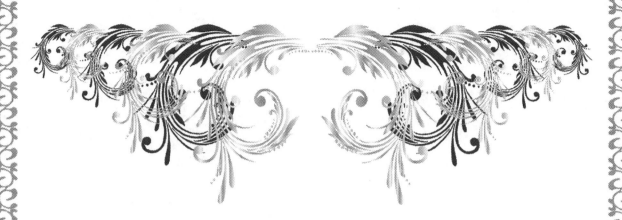

15

در کارگه کوزه گری بودم دوش
دیدم دو هزار کوزه گویای خموش
هر یک به زبان حال با من می‌گفت
کو کوزه‌گر و کوزه‌خر و کوزه فروش

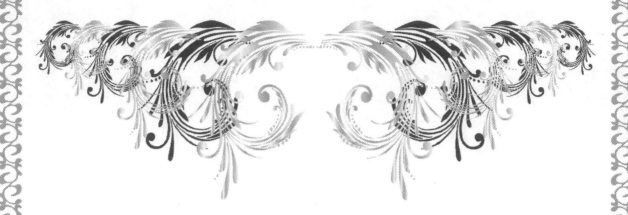

16

Such cup makes the mind bow to its knees

To its cheek hundred of glorified kisses one gives

This worldly potter forms such an exalted cup

Then into the ground, he shatters it up

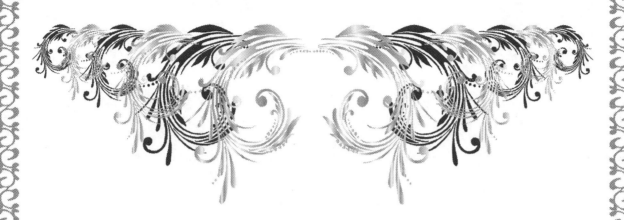

16

جامی است که عقل آفرین می زندش

صد بوسه مهر بر جبین می‌زندش

این کوزه گر دهر چنین جام لطیف

می‌سازد و باز بر زمین می‌زندش

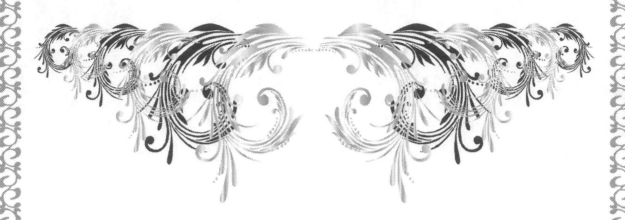

17

Be joyful, for the world will be by passing

Self from the body, will be in rage howling

This head cups, for you see tomorrow

Under the kick of potters, it will forego

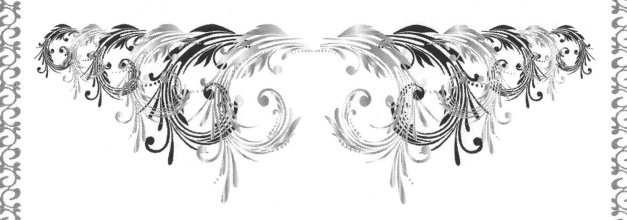

17

خوش باش که عالم گذران خواهد بود

جان در پی تن نعره زنان خواهد بود

این کاسه سرها که تو بینی فردا

زیر لگد کوزه گران خواهد بود

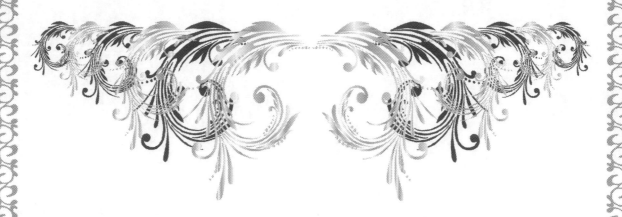

18

Those who became centre to virtue and discipline, amaze

Within perfection a whole, to disciples a blaze

The course of this dark night they did not lead to day

Said a few fantasies and then slept away

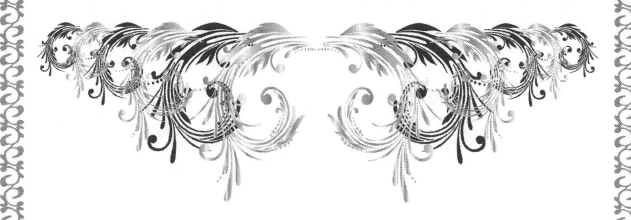

18

آنان که محیط فضل و آداب شدند

در جمع کمال شمع اصحاب شدند

ره زین شب تاریک نبردند به روز

گفتند فسانه‌ای و در خواب شدند

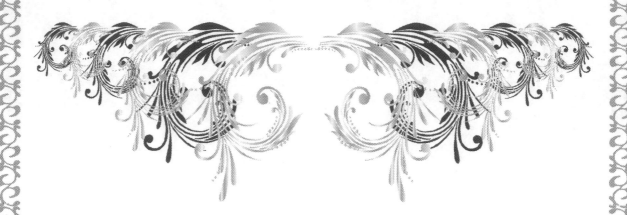

19

This sea of being from the hidden, a disclose

To this pearl, there is none with a delve to enclose

Each one to a covenant, a word foretell

But on the face, what is, no one can tell

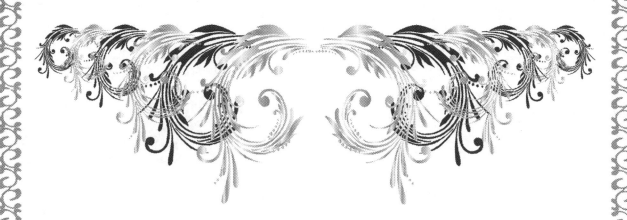

19

این بحر وجود آمده بیرون ز نهفت

کس نیست که این گوهر تحقیق بسفت

هر کس سخنی از سر سودا گفتند

زان روی که هست کس نمی داند گفت

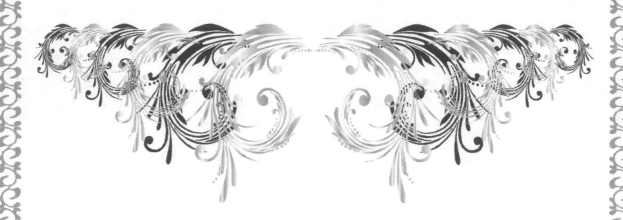

20

The veil of mysteries, no one of it has a way

In this scheme, the soul of no one awareness convey

Except in earth's heart, no other resting place exist

Drink up wine, that such myths are not short in list

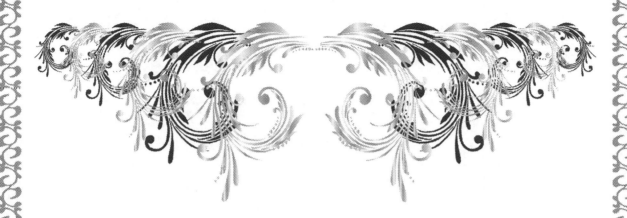

20

در پرده اسرار کسی را ره نیست

زین تعبیه جان هیچکس آگه نیست

جز در دل خاک هیچ منزلگه نیست

می خور که چنین فسانه‌ها کوته نیست

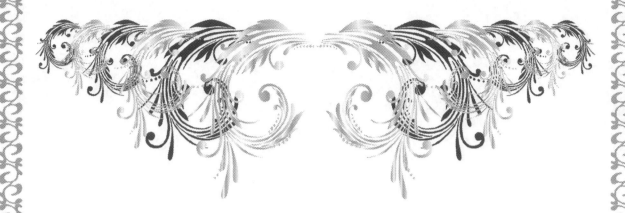

21

From the bundle of wayfarers on this long path

The one returner is where, to tell us the tale's math

Beware heed to this duality as in a dire need

No matters leave aside, for a return comes not indeed

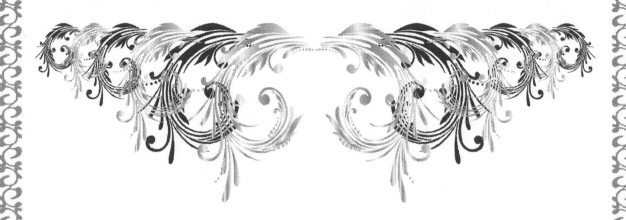

21

از جمله رفتگان این راه دراز

باز آمده ای کو که بما گوید راز

هان برسر این دو راهه از روی نیاز

چیزی نگذاری که نمی‌آیی باز

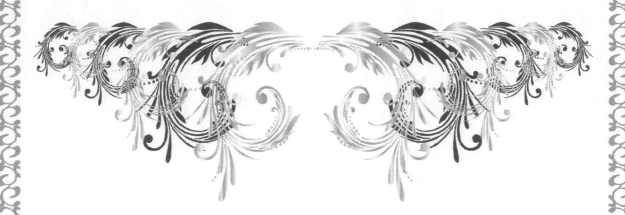

22

Those whom before us departed, oh Cupbearer

In the deceived land, been buried, oh Cupbearer

Go thou, drink wine and hear of me the truth

It's hot air, whatever they've declared, oh Cupbearer

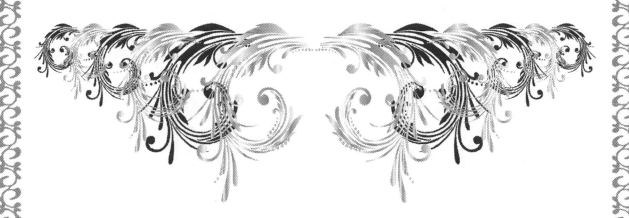

22

آنان که ز پیش رفته‌اند ای ساقی

در خاک غرور خفته‌اند ای ساقی

رو باده خور و حقیقت از من بشنو

باد است هر آن چه گفته‌اند ای ساقی

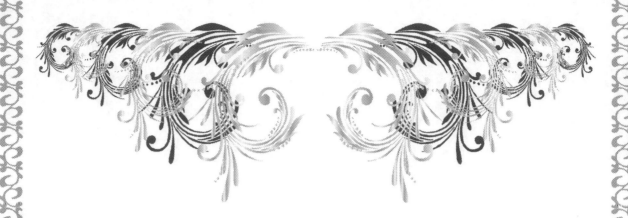

23

Tomorrow, I will the flag of disunion to a roll abridge

With grey hair, wine I will intent a brewage

The measure of my age, to seventy has reached

This moment, if I not joy, when shall joy be reached

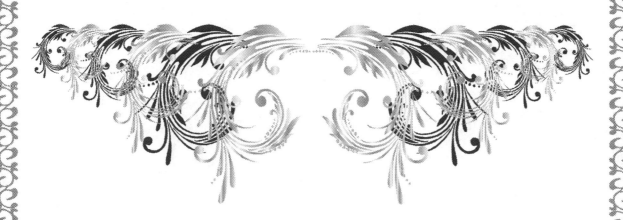

23

فردا علم نفاق طی خواهم کرد

با موی سپید قصد می خواهم کرد

پیمانه عمر من به هفتاد رسید

این دم نکنم نشاط کی خواهم کرد

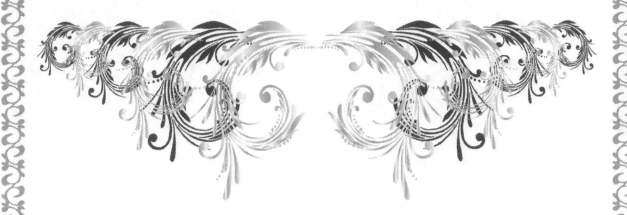

24

Us, liquor, singers, and this ruin world entwine

Self, heart, cup, garment collateral to wine

Hope of mercy, fear of hell, not burdened to bear

Liberated from dust, fire, water and air

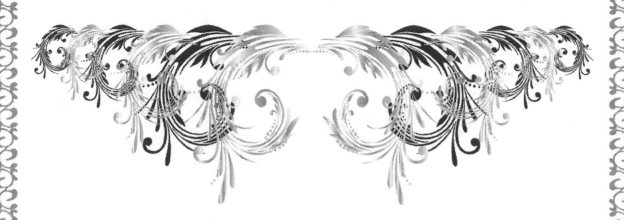

24

ماییم و می و مطرب و این کنج خراب

جان و دل و جام و جامه در رهن شراب

فارغ ز امید و رحمت و بیم و عذاب

آزاد ز خاک و باد و از آتش و آب

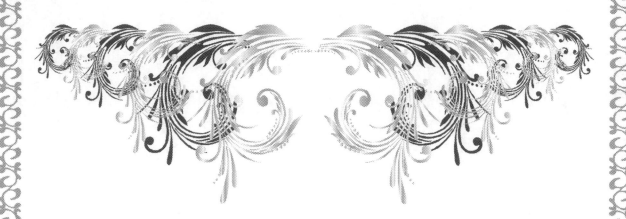

25

The cup of my wine you've Broken, my Lord

Upon me the door of joy you've batten, my Lord

Onto soil you've spilled my pure wine

Pardon my mouth, but were you drunken, my Lord

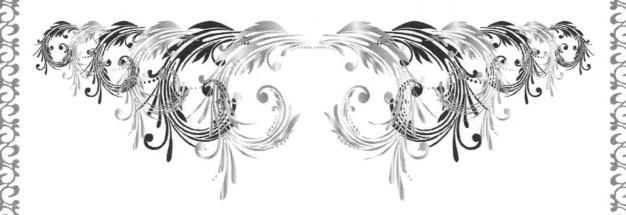

25

ابریق می مرا شکستی ربی

بر من در عیش را بستی ربی

بر خاک بریختی می ناب مرا

خاکم به دهن مگر تو مستی ربی

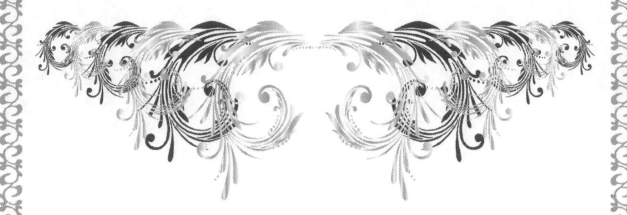

26

Dearest, in friendship as your sights meet

Perhaps that of companions, in memory much greet

Since fine wine you devour and digest conjointly

Turn when comes to us, you invert it wholly

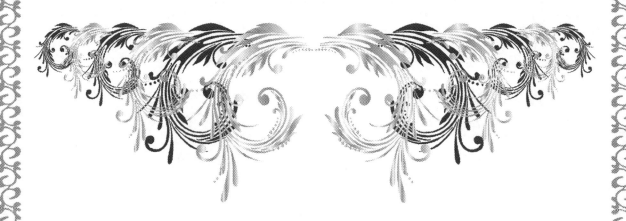

26

یاران به مرافقت چو دیدار کنید

شاید که زدوست یاد بسیار کنید

چون باده خوشگوار نوشید به هم

نوبت چو بما رسد نگونسار کنید

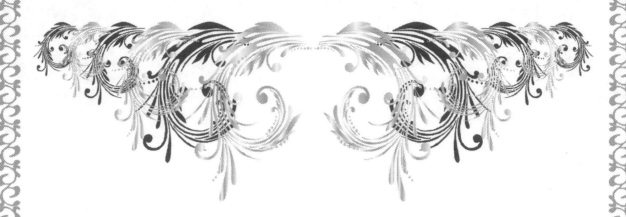

27

I drink wine and whoever like me are aware

My wine drinking to his percept, is a simple affair

My wine drinking, God in eternity to him was known

If wine I don't drink, God's knowledge to ignorance dethrone

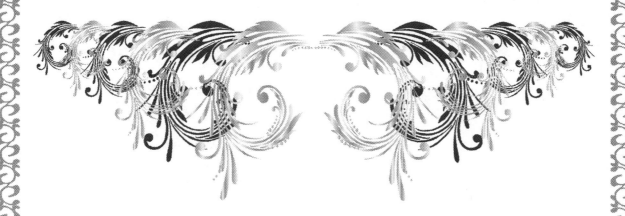

27

من می خورم و هر که چو من اهل بود

می خوردن من به نزد او سهل بود

می خوردن من حق ز ازل می دانست

گر می نخورم علم خدا جهل بود

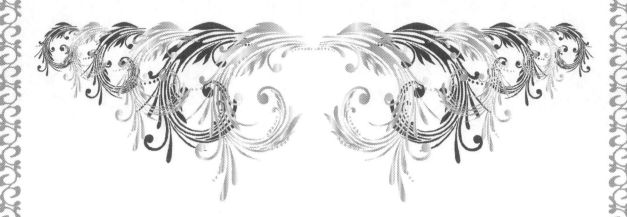

28

Un-committers of sin, say who is it in the world

Those did not commit sin, say how their life twirled

I mischief commit and you mischiefly retaliate

Then a difference between you and I is what, dictate

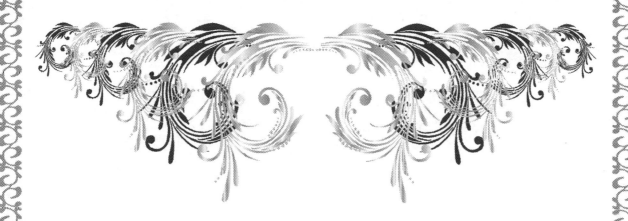

28

ناکرده گناه در جهان کیست بگو

آنکس که گنه نکرد چون زیست بگو

من بد کنم و تو بد مکافات دهی

پس فرق میان من و تو چیست بگو

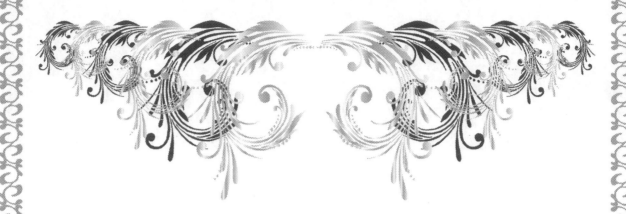

29

Hellish are drunken and lovers, I've been told

A violated vow, can not the heart to it be sold

If lovers and drunken into hell are doomed

Morrow will be heaven like a palm of hand consumed

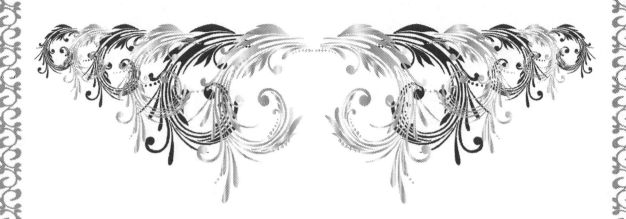

29

گویند که دوزخی بود عاشق و مست

قولی است خلاف دل در آن نتوان بست

گر عاشق ومست دوزخی خواهد بود

فردا باشد بهشت همچون کف دست

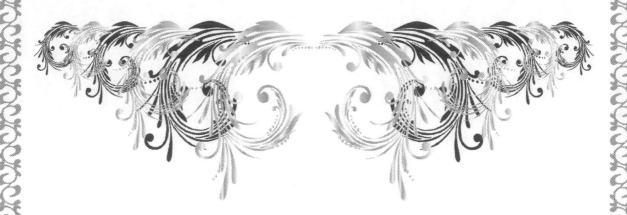

30

With Houri say some, heaven is joyful

I for claim, the juice of grape is joyful

Take this Treasure and relinquish of that credit

As harkening to a sound of drum is from far pleasant

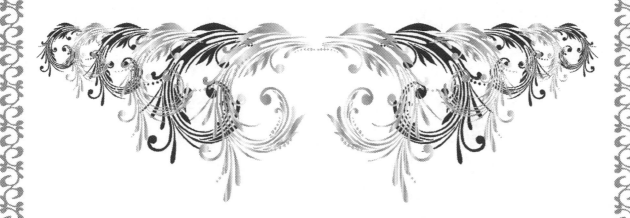

30

گویند بهشت با حور خوش است

من می گویم که آب انگور خوش است

این نقد بگیر و دست از آن نسیه بدار

کاواز دهل شنیدن از دور خوش است

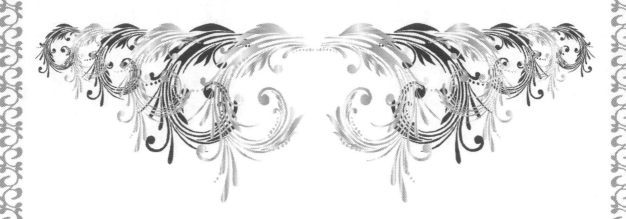

31

Wine drinking and enjoyment is my Religion

free from creed and blasphemy is my conviction

I said to the bride of eternity, quantify your endowment

Said, the flourishing of your heart, is my settlement

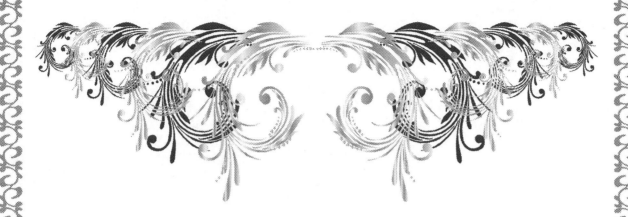

31

می خوردن و شاد بودن آیین منست

فارغ بودن ز کفر و دین؛ دین منست

گفتم به عروس دهر کابین تو چیست

گفتا دل خرم تو کابین من است

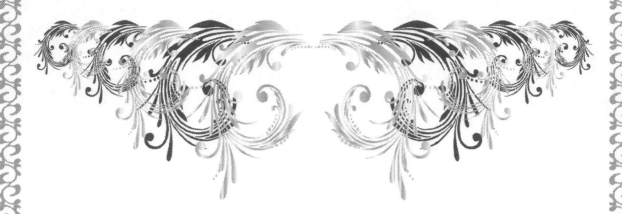

32

A cup of wine, merit hundred of heart and religion

A sip of wine, merit domain of China and its Eden

On the face of earth not there is, but ruby of wine

Its bitterness merit the embody of thousand sweets combine

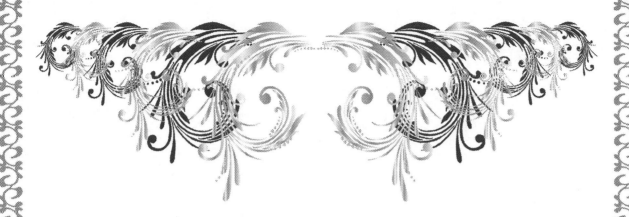

32

یک جام شراب صد دل و دین ارزد

یک جرعه می مملکت چین ارزد

جز باده لعل نیست در روی زمین

تلخی که هزار جان شیرین ارزد

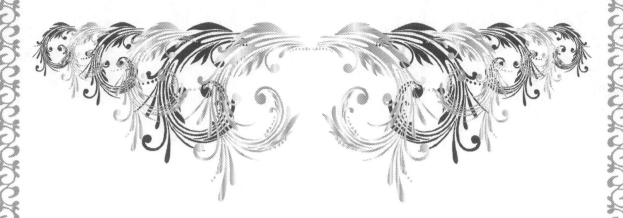

33

The iniquity I have, the backbone of faith it breaks

The bright trade of the idolaters it breaks

The load of my sin, if by the scale measured

I fear in judgement day, the scale by it breaks

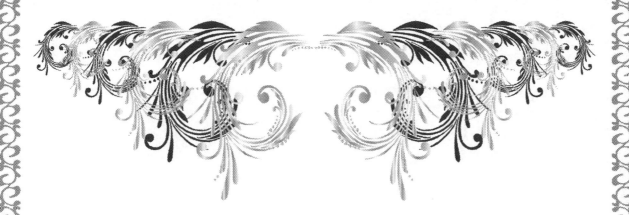

33

دارم گنهی که پشت ایمان شکند

بازار تمام بت پرستان شکند

بار گنهم اگر بمیزان سنجد

ترسم که بروز حشر میزان شکند

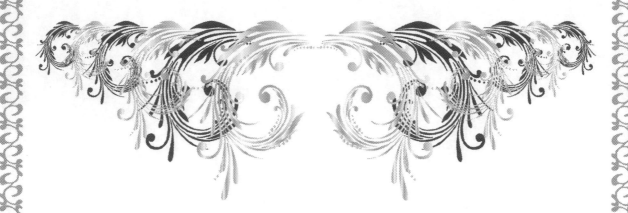

34

My wine drinking is not for excitement

Not to cut out creed, manner nor for enjoyment

I want to be away from myself for a moment

My drinking and tipsiness for that cause is apparent

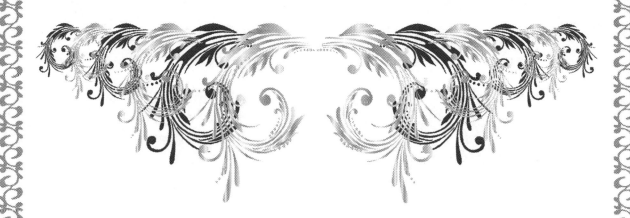

34

می خوردن من نه از برای طربست

نز بهر نشاط و ترک دین و ادبست

خواهم که دمی ز خویشتن باز رهم

می خوردن و مست بودنم زین سبب است

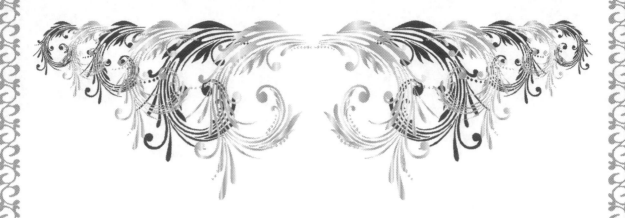

35

This caravan of life, in stun it bypasses

Comprehend for an instance, in delight it bypasses

Cupbearer, worrying about morrow's hustlers what for

Bring forth the Cup, for the night is passing in soar

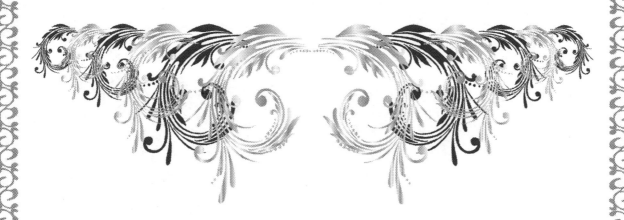

35

این قافله عمر عجب می گذرد

دریاب دمی که با طرب می گذرد

ساقی غم فردای حریفان چه خوری؟

پیش آر پیاله را که شب می‌گذرد

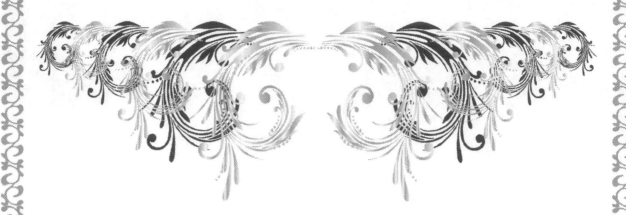

36

Oh longing that a place of relaxation you had been

Or to this distant road a destination you had been

Longing, after thousands of years from earth's heart

Like greenery, a hope of an emanation you had been

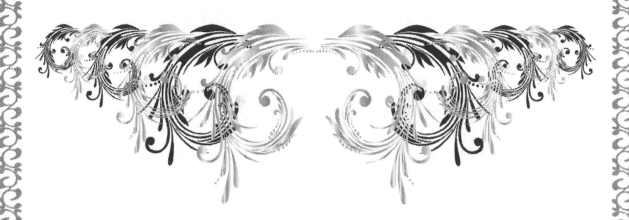

36

ای کاش که جای آرمیدن بودی

یا این ره دور را رسیدن بودی

کاش از پی صد هزار سال از دل خاک

چون سبزه امید بر دمیدن بودی

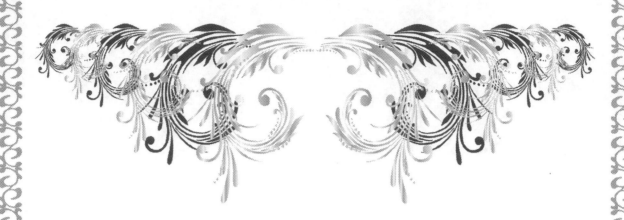

37

Cupbearer, my grief grand is its melody

My awareness is, beyond its boundary

With grey hair, drunk I am from your wine

In old age, heart to spring renew align

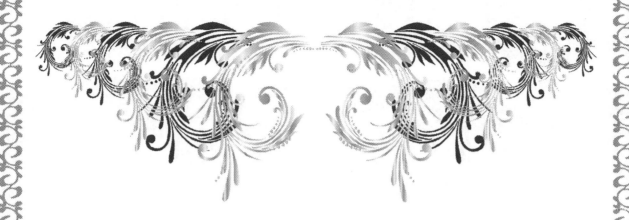

37

ساقی غم من بلند آوازه شده است

بیداری من برون ز اندازه شده‌است

با موی سپید سرخوشم از می تو

پیرانه سرم بهار دل تازه شده است

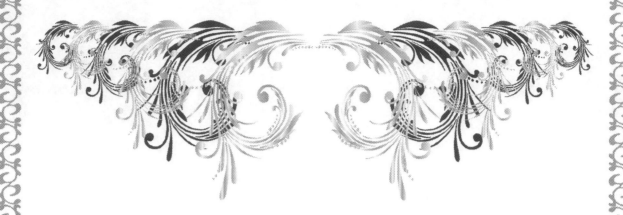

38

Cupbearer, the flower and greenery have over bloomed

Comprehend, within a week's time to dust they're consumed

Devour wine and pluck a flower, till of it you observe

The flower to dust and greenery to motes swerve

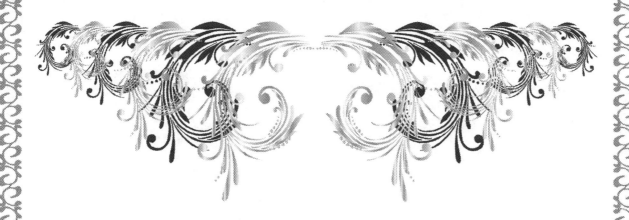

38

ساقی ، گل و سبزه بس طربناک شده است

دریاب که هفته دگر خاکشده است

می نوش و گلی بچین که تادر نگری

گل خاک شده است سبزه خاشاک شده است

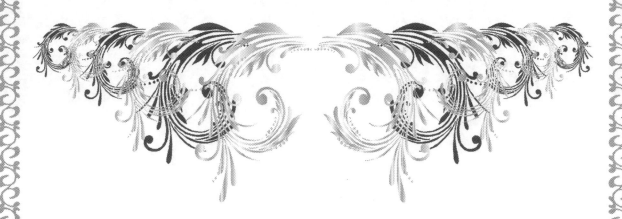

39

Till when do I worry whether I have or not
This life to be spend joyously or not
Fill up the bowl of wine, for I am unsure
This breath I inhale, whether I exhale it or not

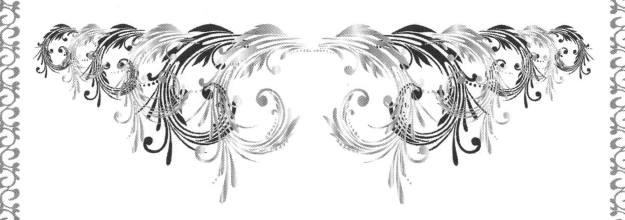

39

تا کی غم آن خورم که دارم یا نه

وین عمر به خوشدلی گذارم یا نه

پر کن قدح باده که معلومم نیست

این دم که فرو برم برآرام یا نه

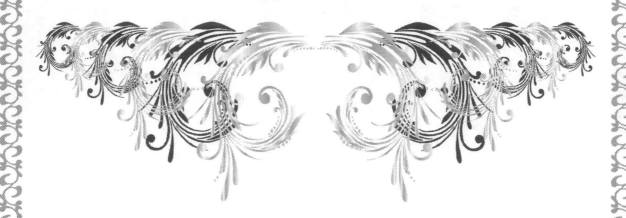

40

Those off guard that to the pearl meaning dwelled

About the cosmos all sort of assertions, have impelled

Aware as they were not, to secret of the world

First triviality they hit and lastly to sleep curled

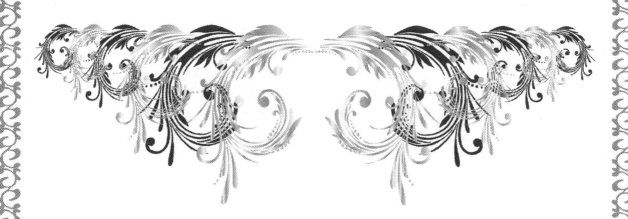

40

آن بی‌خبران که در معنی سفتند

در چرخ به انواع سخن‌ها گفتند

آگه چو نگشتند بر اسرار جهان

اول ز نخی زدند و آخر خفتند

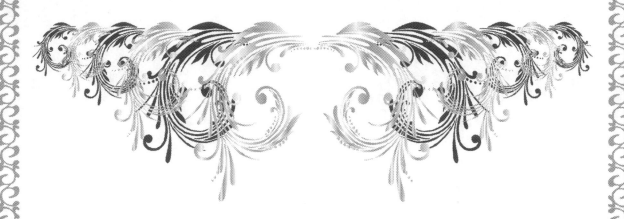

41

Some people's contemplation is within religion

Some are certain, in the path of illusion

I fear of that, when a call comes a day

Oh unaware the path is neither way

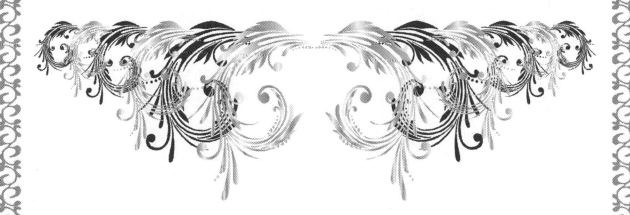

41

قومی متفکرند اندر ره دین

قومی به گمان فتاده در راه یقین

می‌ترسم از آنکه بانگ آید روزی

کی بیخبران راه نه آن است و نه این

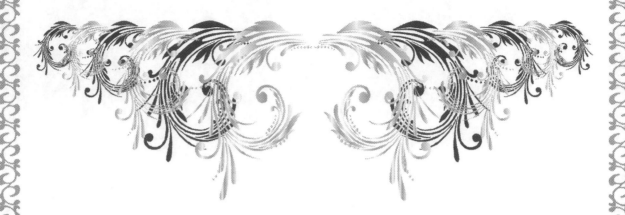

42

Oh those who are a result of four and seven
Of seven and four always in a confine liven
Devour wine, you a thousand times I've told upon
There is no return, as you're gone you're gone

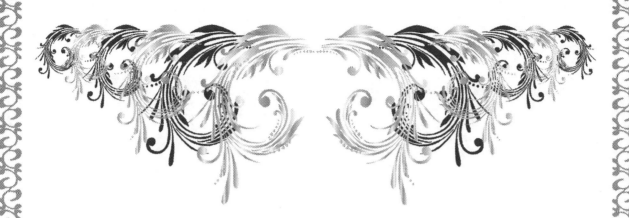

42

ای آن که نتیجه چهار و هفتی

وز هفت و چهار دایم اندر تفتی

می‌خور که هزار باره بیش ات گفتم

باز آمدنت نیست چو رفتی، رفتی

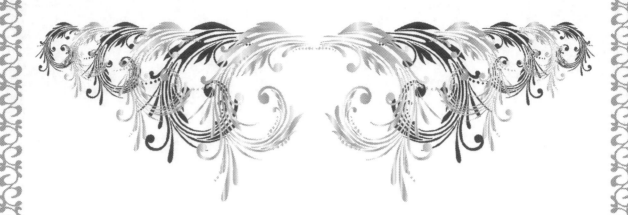

43

Oh who, have arrived heated, from the world of spirit

Perplexed in four, six, seven and eight you audit

Devour wine for its unknown from where you emanate

Be joyful, for its unknown, where you will eventuate

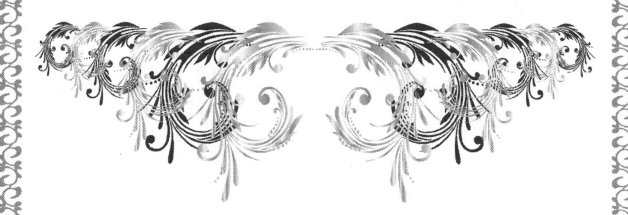

43

اي آمده از عالم روحاني تفت

حيران شده در پنج وچهار وشش وهفت

مي نوش نداني ز كجا آمده‌اي

خوش باش نداني بكجا خواهي رفت

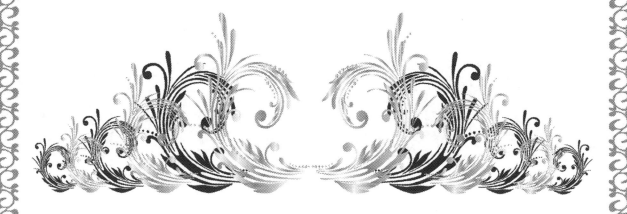

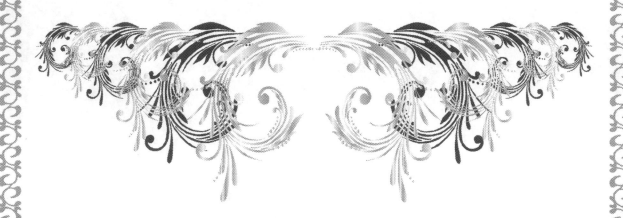

44

The essence of being and nothingness I attained

The innermost essence of highs and lows I attained

Still bashful, with all that I attained

If a state beyond drunkenness can be obtained

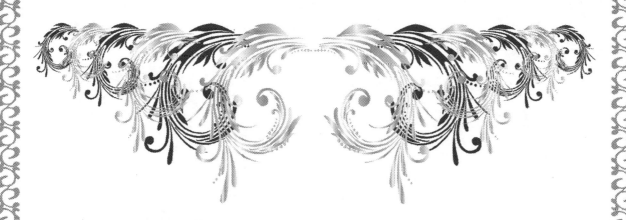

44

من ظاهر نیستی و هستی دانم

من باطن هر فراز و پستی دانم

با این همه از دانش خود شرمم باد

گر مرتبه ای ورای مستی دانم

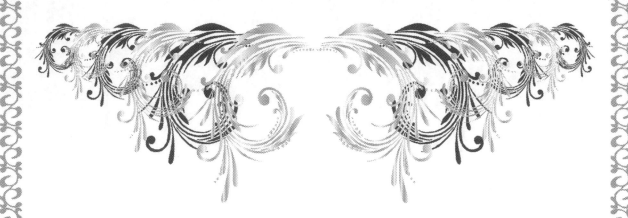

45

We are the puppets and cosmos the puppeteer

In the face of reality, not in a face to metaphor peer

A while in this ribbing we played

Falling in a chest of nihility, in turn we fade

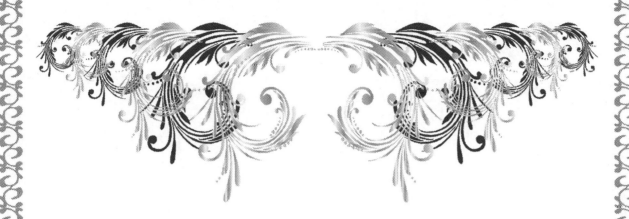

45

ما لعبتکانیم و فلک لعبت باز

از روی حقیقتی نه از روی مجاز

یک چند در این بساط بازی کردیم

رفتیم به صندوق عدم یک یک باز

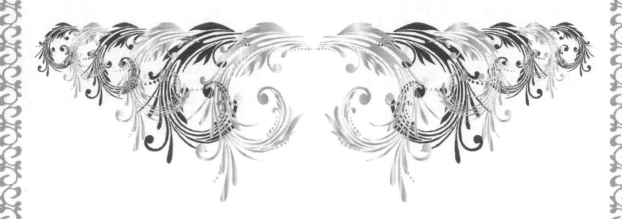

46

As life passes by, whether Bagdad or Balkh the Same

As a cup full, whether bitter or sweet the same

Be joyful, after you and I, the moon selfsame

Many times its orbit east to west will reclaim

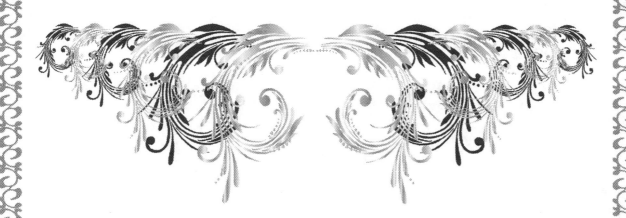

46

چون عمر بسر رسد چه بغداد و چه بلخ

پیمانه چو پر شود چه شیرین و چه تلخ

خوش باش که بعد از من و تو ماه بسی

از سلخ به غره آید از غره به سلخ

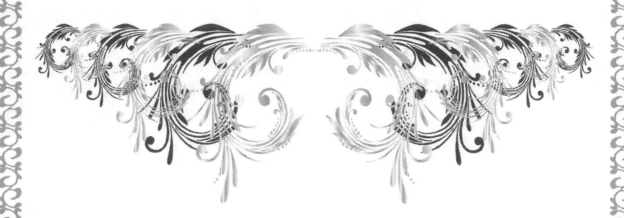

47

Your age whether a hundred or thousand years

In this ancient world, your expelling adheres

If a king you are, or a beggar in the market

This two, by the same value its end plummet

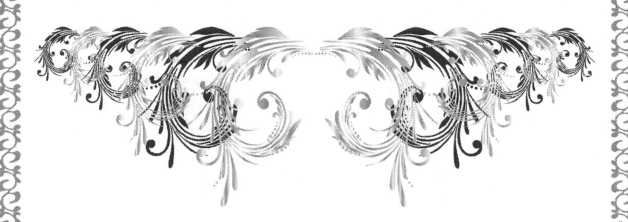

47

عمرت چو دو صد بود چه سیصد چه هزار

زین کهنه سرای برون برندت ناچار

گر پادشهی و گر گدای بازار

این هر دو بیک نرخ بود آخر کار

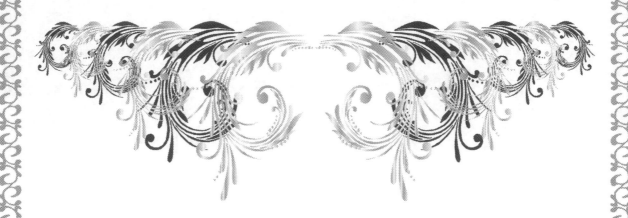

48

Cosmos is a glance, to our withered body

Oxus is the trace, of our tears strained daily

Hell is the agony of our hollow longing

Heaven is a glimpse of our brief resting

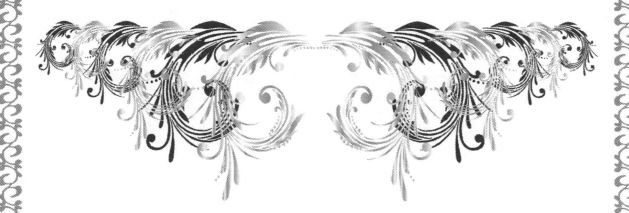

48

گردون نگری ز قد فرسوده ماست

جیحون اثری ز اشک پالوده ماست

دوزخ شرری ز رنج بیهوده ماست

فردوس دمی ز وقت آسوده ماست

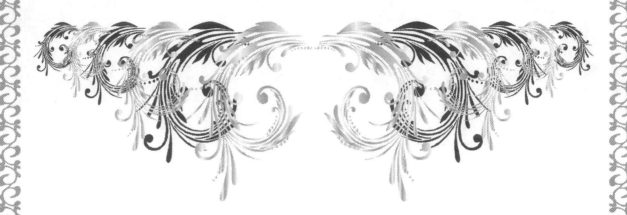

49

As good and evil, within self, are contained

Joy and sorrow, as in fate and destiny sustained

With cosmos, do not bargain by intellectual

As cosmos is far more than you ineffectual

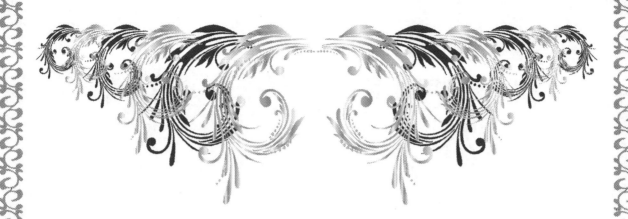

49

نیکی و بدی که در نهاد بشر است

شادی و غمی که در قضا و قدر است

با چرخ مکن حواله کاندر ره عقل

چرخ از تو هزار بار بیچاره تر است

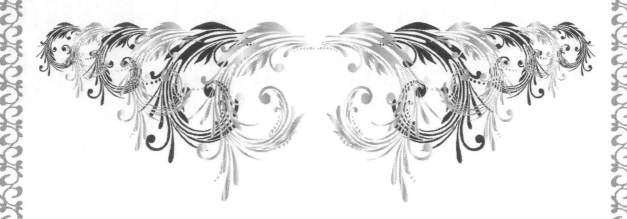

50

Oh heart, as the truth of world is mere speculation

How far to degrade from this everlasting tribulation

Submit the body to fate, and tune with inflict

As this set out pen, for the sake of you, will not revert

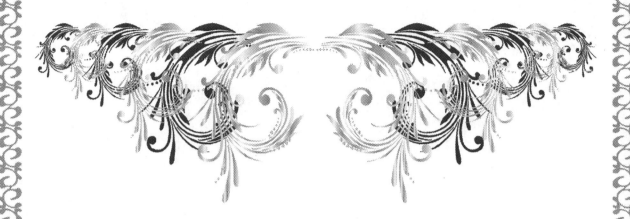

50

ای دل چو حقیقت جهان هست مجاز

چندین چه بری خواری ازین رنج دراز

تن را به قضا سپار و با درد بساز

کاین رفته قلم ز بهر تو ناید باز

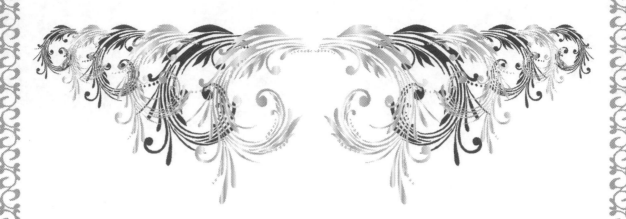

51

As your death is a death once and for all

Once and for all die, this what sort of a befall

Blood, filth, skin, a few veins and artery

As if there never was, this what sort of a misery

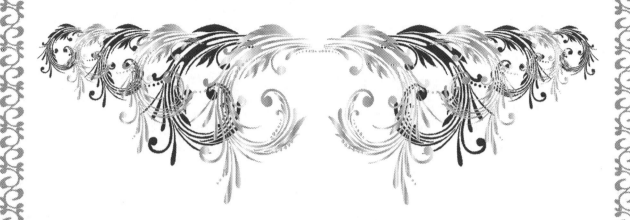

51

چون مردن تو مردن بیکبارگی است

یکبار بمیر این چه بیچارگی است

خونی ونجاستی و مشتی رگ و پوست

انگار نبود این چه غمخوارگی است

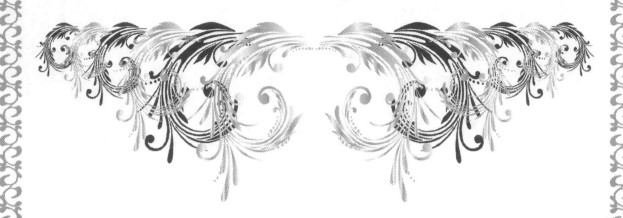

52

In me a fortitude to the cupbearer's strife remained

In the people's chit chat, Insincerity are contained

Of the last night's wine, no more than a cup sustained

Of life I don't know, how much of it have remained

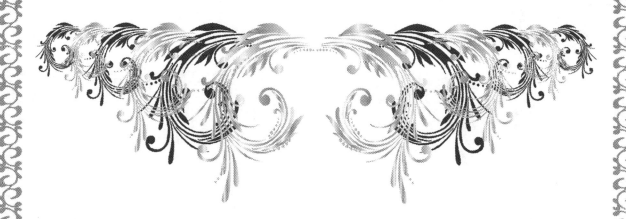

52

از مـن رمقی بـه سعی سـاقی مانده است

وز صحبت خلق بی وفایی مانده است

از بـاده دوشـین قـدحی بـیش نـمـاند

از عمر نـدانم که چه باقی مانده است

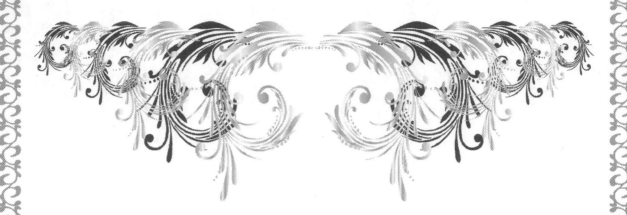

53

Since arriving was not in my hand the first day

This undesired departure, is it right the last day

Rise and tight up oh Cupbearer at once, don't betray

As with wine, I'll wash the world's sorrows away

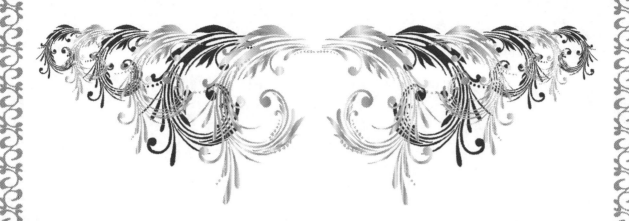

53

چون آمدنم به من نبد روز نخست

وین رفتن بی مراد عزمی ست درست

بر خیز و میان ببند ای ساقی چست

کاندوه جهان به می فرو خواهم شست

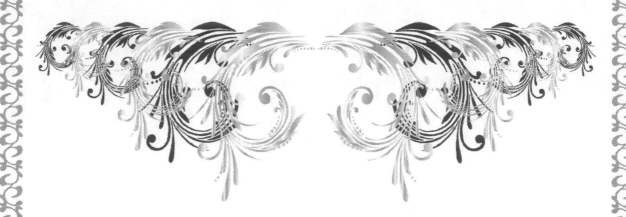

54

The cycle which in it our coming and going appear

Of this, neither the end nor the beginning is clear

None an utter gave, a breath to its implication true

That this coming is from where and the going is where to

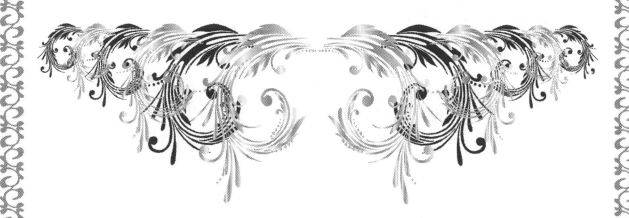

54

دوری که در او آمدن و رفتن ماست

او را نه نهایت نه بدایت پیداست

کس می نزند دمی درین معنی راست

کاین آمدن از کجا و رفتن به کجاست

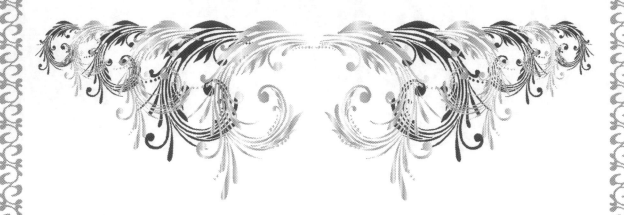

55

Oh friend come, for worry of tomorrow not to intake

This one breath of life, cherish its spoils for keepsake

Tomorrow, from this ancient haunt as we transmute

With seven thousand years we are to commute

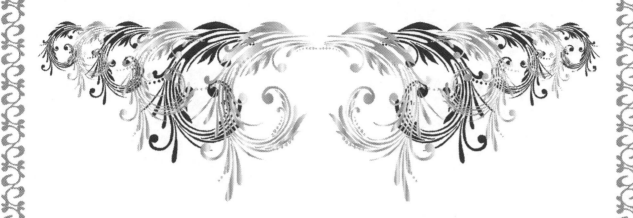

55

ای دوست بیا تا غم فردا نخوریم

وین یکدم عمر را غنیمت شمریم

فردا که ازین دیر کهن در گذریم

با هفت هزار سالگان سر بسریم

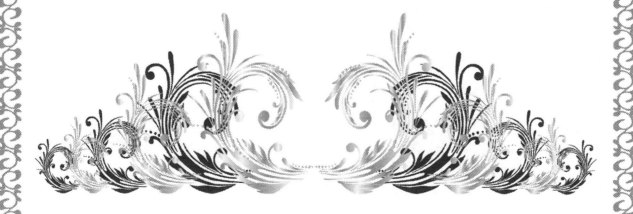

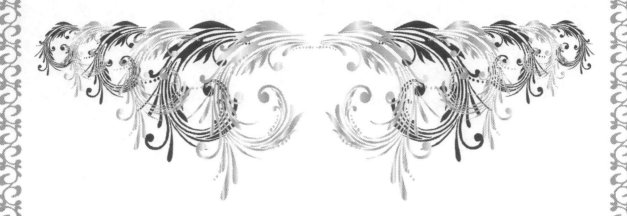

56

Drink wine as under mud for long you'll be buried

Without intimate, friends, companion and married

Cautious, to no one this hidden truth uncover

That each tulip fades it won't glow and recover

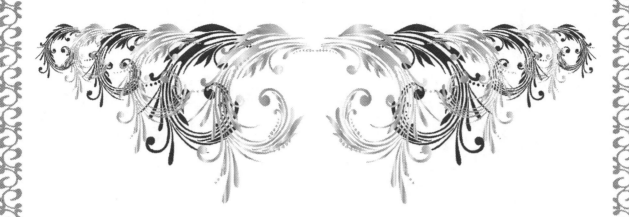

56

می خور که به زیر گل بسی خواهی خفت

بی مونس و بی رفیق و بی همدم و جفت

زنهار به کس مگو تو این راز نهفت

هر لاله که پژمرد نخواهد بشکفت

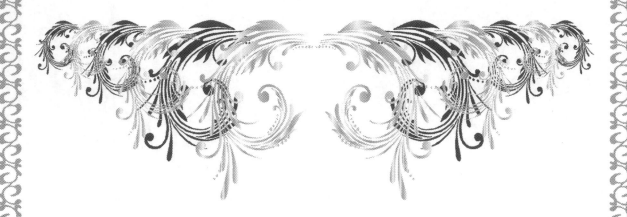

57

Until the hands of unity in row are not composed

The step of joy upon grief will not be disposed

Us rising and taking a breath, before the morn's moment

As the morn much breaths, which we to the breathing absent

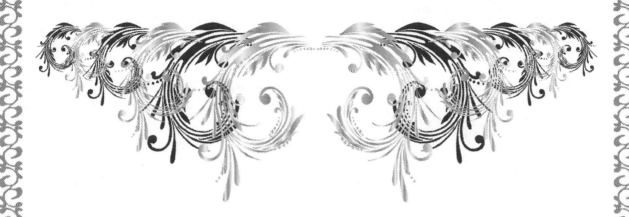

57

تا دست به اتفاق بر هم نزنیم

پایی ز نشاط بر سر هم نزنیم

خیزیم و دمی زنیم پیش از دم صبح

کاین صبح بسی دمد که ما دم نزنیم

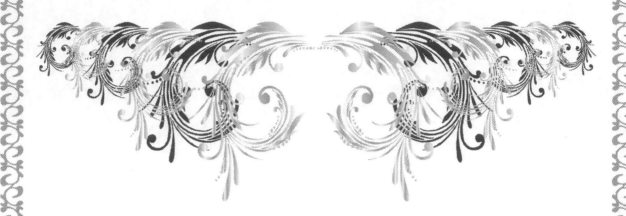

58

A love, that is a figure like, not there to it a climax

Such as a fire half dead, brightness to it, ever more lacks

A lover must, to year, month, night and day

calm, stable, dining, sleeping, not have a way

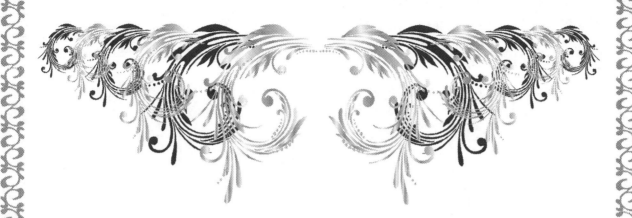

58

عشقی که مجازی بود آبش نبود

چون آتش نیم مرده تابش نبود

عاشق باید که سال و ماه و شب و روز

آرام و قرار و خورد و خوابش نبود

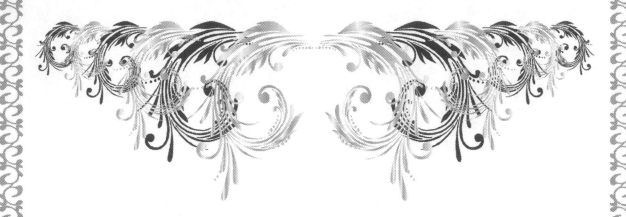

59

It's morning, a moment with a rosy wine let's spend

This bottle of names and shames by stone put to an end

Withdrawing   our   hand   from   endure   craving

In a long ringlet of harp and to its skirt embracing

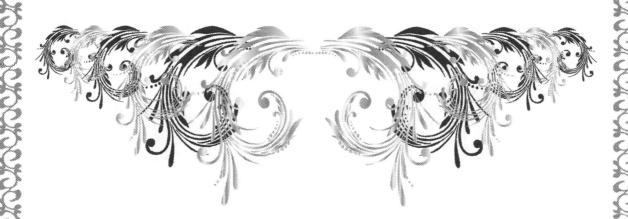

59

صبح است دمی بر می گلرنگ زنیم

وین شیشه نام و ننگ بر سنگ زنیم

دست از عمل دراز خود باز کشیم

در زلف دراز و دامن چنگ زنیم

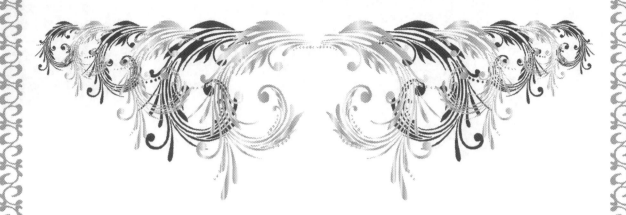

60

Cycle of the world, it's nothing without Cupbearers and wine

It's nothing without murmur of Iraqi's melody shrine

The more I look and observe the world congest

All to yield is feasting, it's nothing all the rest

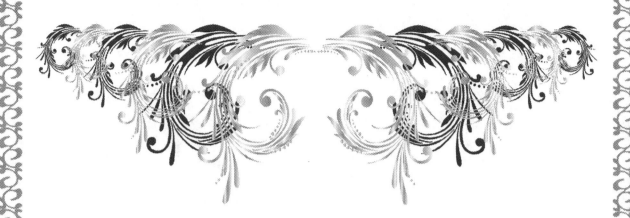

60

دوران جهان بی می و ساقی هیچ است

بی زمزمه ساز عراقی هیچ است

هر چند در احوال جهان می نگرم

حاصل همه عشرت است و باقی هیچ است

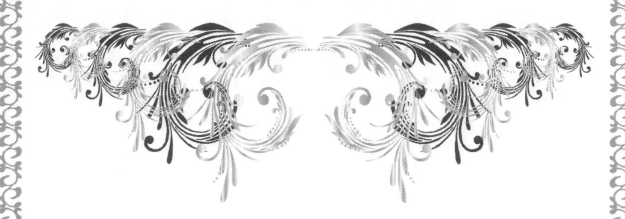

61

I'm proud of Tavern, for its belongers belong

With fair as you observe, simple are its wrong

In School did not up rise, any belonger of heart

Ruin be on this place, for it's an ignorance mart

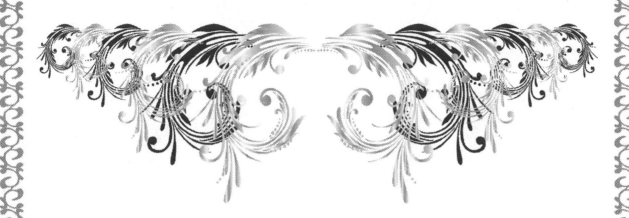

61

نازم به خرابات که اهلش اهل است

چون نیک نظر کنی بدش هم سهل است

از مدرسه بر نخواست هیچ اهل دلی

ویران شود این خرابه دارالجهل است

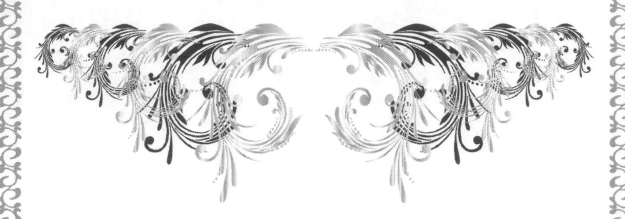

62

Oh mufti of town, than you more to work we strive

With all this tipsiness, than you more alert we contrive

You blood in others drain, and we drain blood in grape

Be fair to this, which one of us to parasite's thirst, a shape

---

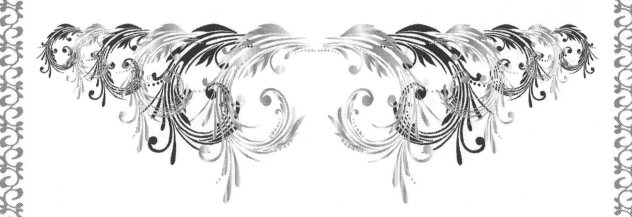

62

ای مفتــــــی شهـــــــر از تـــو پرکارتریم

بــا ایــن همـــه مستی ز تــو هشیارتـریم

تـو خــون کســان نوشـــی و مـا خـون رزان

انصـــــاف بـــــده کـــــدام خونخــوارتریم

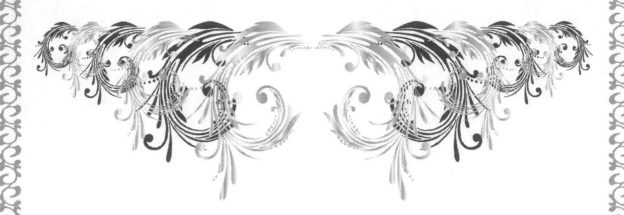

63

A cunning one I saw, he was sitting over stupid land

No blasphemy, no Islam, no religion, no worldly stand

No truth, no right, no dogma, no conviction

Within both worlds, who to this courage, a liken

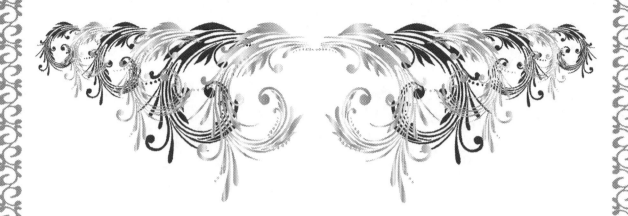

63

رندی دیدم نشسته بر خنگ زمین

نه کفر و نه اسلام و نه دنیا و نه دین

نی حق نه حقیقت نه شریعت نه یقین

اندر دو جهان کرا بود زهره این

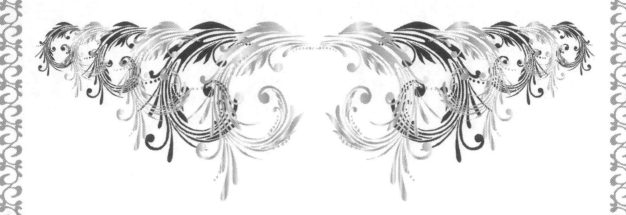

64

Khayyam if by wine you're drunk, be joyful

By moonlight beauty if you're beside, be joyful

As aftermath of world deed is nonexistence

As it were you never existed, but since you exist, be joyful

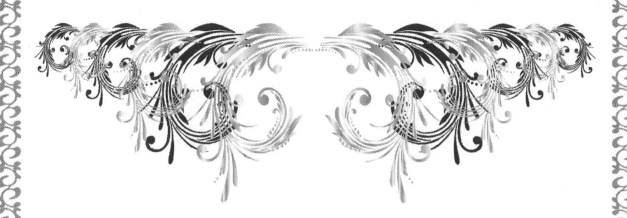

64

خیام اگر ز باده مستی خوش باش

با ماه رخی اگر نشستی خوش باش

چون عاقبت کار جهان نیستی است

انگار که نیستی چو هستی خوش باش

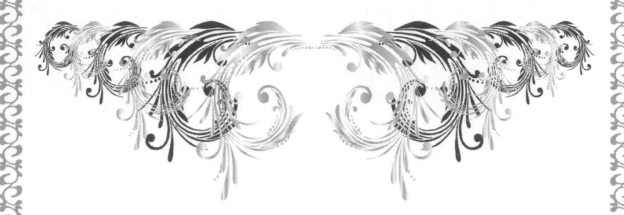

65

Days that have passed, of it again don't reminiscence

Tomorrow that has not arrived, don't a clamour presence

Of yet not arrived and of the past don't build a base

For the present be happy and life in vain don't unlace

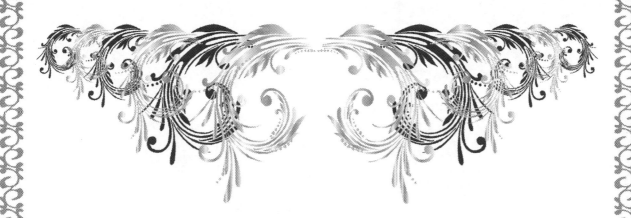

65

روزی که گذشت از او دگر یاد مکن

فردا که نیامدست فریاد مکن

بر نامده و گذشته بنیاد مکن

حالی خوش باش و عمر بر باد مکن